FLOAT

Other titles in the series

Baits
Rods and Reels
Hooks, Lines and Knots

FLOAT AND LEGER RIGS
for coarse fishing

By Ken Whitehead
Illustrated by Russell Birkett

WARD LOCK

© Text and illustrations Ward Lock Limited 1989

First published in Great Britain in 1989
by Ward Lock Limited, 8 Clifford Street
London W1X 1RB

Designed by Bob Vickers
Text filmset in Times
by Litho Link Ltd, Welshpool, Powys

Printed and bound in Great Britain

British Library Cataloguing in Publication Data
Whitehead, Ken, *1930 Aug. 10 —*
   Float and leger rigs for coarse fishing. —
   (Fishing skills pocket book).
   1. Coarse fish. Angling
   I. Title II. Series
   799.1′1

   ISBN 0-7063-6827-4

CONTENTS

Preface   7

Floats: Introduction   9
The Water   12
The Weather   14
The Fish   15
Casting   16
The Light   16
Adaptability   17
Storing floats   23
Making floats   23

Float patterns   25
Quills   25
Avon floats   26
Balsa floats   28
Stick floats   28
Waggler floats   30
Slider floats   35
Antennae floats   36
Bubble floats   37
Pole floats   38
Night lights   40
Bungs   41

Weights for float fishing   43
Weighting patterns   45

Float-fishing styles   46
Trotting   47
Laying-on   48

Stret-pegging   50
Lift method   51
Drop method   52
Sink-and-draw   54
Sliding-float rigs   56
Stick-floats   57
Wagglers   58
Float paternoster   63
Pole float rigs   64

Swimfeeders   67

Pike-fishing rigs   70

Leger rigs   73
Leger weights   74
Leger stops   77
Static leger   80
Rolling leger   81
Link leger   82
Long-range leger   82
Link leger   82
Fixed-link leger   83
Swimfeeder legering   84
Paper-bag legering   84
Swan-shot legering   85
Detecting bites   86
Touch legering   86
Rod rests   87
Butt indicators   88
Swingtips   89
Quivertips   89

Index   91

PREFACE

It is safe to say that every coarse angler starts his career by fishing with a float and it is only some time later that there comes the understanding that there is another method called legering.

In this volume of the series the float in its various forms is discussed and the conditions under which each one is used. Water, weather and fish species all play their part in arriving at the most useful float for the session ahead.

The second part of the book deals with fishing without a float: legering. There are some water conditions where the use of a float is nigh impossible, or where the feeding habits of the fish species sought necessitate the bait being on the bottom.

The author of this series, Ken Whitehead, is an all-round fisherman versed in both float fishing and legering, depending on the species found in the water he happens to be fishing. His biggest fish is a pike well in excess of 30 lb and he can include carp in the early 20s among the many entries in his fishing diary. He has come to feel that while the pike's lifestyle includes the taking of live fish, the use of livebaiting is not for him.

He has written or co-authored over 20 books covering every aspect of the sport and was one of the innovators of the pictorial approach to teaching new and would-be anglers the tricks of the trade.

Ken Whitehead is as keen on shooting and the countryside in general as he is on fishing and contributes to several magazines. His first shooting book is due to be published this year.

The artist responsible for the clear, no-nonsense black-and-white drawings is 23-year-old Russell Birkett a young graduate with a BA(Hons) degree in Graphic Information and Design from Falmouth. The illustrations in this series are his first major contribution to the field of book illustration and he intends to pursue a career in publishing. He lives in Eastbourne, Sussex.

Len Cacutt, general editor of the series, has been closely concerned with angling publishing in all its forms, having himself written a number of books and compiled and edited angling books, magazines and encyclopedias for the leading publishers, and was Founder Editor of an angling newspaper. He has acted as angling adviser and consultant to a number of publishing houses.

INTRODUCTION: FLOATS

That most anglers use a float when they fish is not surprising: the float is a focal point where action might occur, the means of knowing when a fish is interested in the bait and – even more important – a final indication that the bait has been taken into the fish's mouth, the moment to strike. Most anglers use a float because of the ease with which it records the bite. The float leger, the pure leger and even free-lining are equally efficient styles in catching fish, but their use demands more skill from the angler in recognising a bite, then assessing what the fish is doing with the bait.

Some anglers go through their fishing lives using only two or three types of float to cover every need, regardless of the water being fished, the species sought or the season and it is a recipe for disaster. The float to be used must be decided on after a number of facts have been examined and considered. On the other hand there is no need for the vast array of floats one sees in the tackle shops or occasionally beside the angler at the waterside.

Is the float really necessary? Some of the reasons have been given above, the most important being that the float records a bite from a fish. But that is not all. For instance, it is often possible to identify the fish that is interested in the bait. The dashing, grabbing bite of a perch is one example: the sudden lift, then collapse of the float horizontally on the surface, followed by a lift and slow drag under is the unmistakable hallmark of a bream bite. Lightning stabs at the float usually indicate a dace, while there is no mistaking the sucking, delicate bite from a tench, making the float slowly wobble and gyrate. With this knowledge the angler soon knows that it is not necessary to strike immediately at the first twitch of the float, sometimes it is prudent to wait on the alert for the fish to swim away with the bait.

So, by studying float movements a picture can be built up of what is happening under the surface. In simple terms, the float records attention. This attention is sometimes unwelcome, as when a small nuisance perch pulls at the bait, the hook or line becomes caught on the bottom, or on an underwater snag, but again the angler soon recognises this as something separate from a bite and reacts accordingly.

Just as important as indicating attention is the ability of the float to carry and direct a bait. There are several ways in which this can be done and the angler must take full advantage of them. For instance, the float can hold a bait clear of the bottom, which will prevent snagging, perhaps tangling in weed; more usually the float holds the bait so that it can be recognised as edible and taken by a fish.

A float can use the current to carry the bait to where the angler considers a fish to be lying. Swimming the stream, where the float (with the baited hook) is carried along with the current, is an example. By holding the line back, or by moving the rod tip, the angler can manoeuvre the float – and with it the bait – to reach specific areas, such as underwater roots close to the bank where a fish may be lying.

Finally, the wind can be used to move the float and carry a bait. This is particularly useful in stillwaters where even a small float, together with the line, will sweep a bait into a place inaccessible to the angler by normal casting. Recently, pike anglers have been taking advantage of the wind and special floats with adjustable and interchangeable sails have been produced that will drift a balanced bait across large distances.

Recording a bite is not the only piece of underwater information that the float gives. It also informs the angler of the exact location of the bait – and that information can be invaluable. Perhaps an underwater hot-spot has been found, say a ridge or hole where fish are lying and where they are interested in feeding. It is the float and its position which tells the angler whether the cast has been successful or not.

In a similar way the float provides information about a hooked fish while it is being played, especially when fishing in deep water. With the float above the surface the direction it takes can show where a fish is heading and approximately how far it is below the surface.

On arrival at the bank and intending to use a float, the angler should stop and think, not reach blindly for that old favourite, or one regarded as a lucky charm.

The Water

Whether the water has movement or not will influence the type of float to be selected. If the water is still, the first consideration must be a small float that will land quietly on the water and present little or no resistance to a taking fish. If the water is moving, strength of current will dictate the size of float to be used.

If the intention is to lay-on, or hold a float still in the current a slim float must be selected. For trotting, allowing the float to ride along with the current, a float substantial in length and circumference will be needed to pull line from the reel.

With depth, movement must be also be considered. Using a large float in shallow water is counter-productive. Colour of the water is also a consideration: in gin-clear streams the float above the bait can be seen. (1)

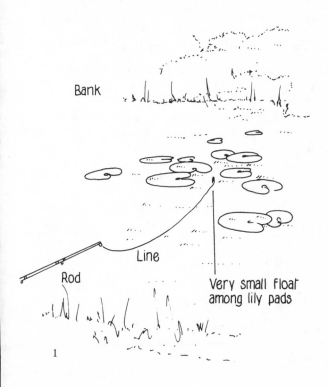

Bank

Line

Rod

Very small float
among lily pads

1

The Weather

Wind and rain are the float fisherman's two main enemies, both making casting difficult and, by disturbing the surface of the water, creating problems with visibility and drag. Again, the angler must select the float to suit the occasion. A heavy float and the weight necessary to cock it will prevent line cling (nylon sticking to the surface of the rod) and help to achieve distance when the cast is made.

The angler's visibility can be assisted in difficult conditions by the use of windbeaters, floats with a small round knob or beacon on their tips which stand high above the surface of the water and can be seen for a considerable distance.

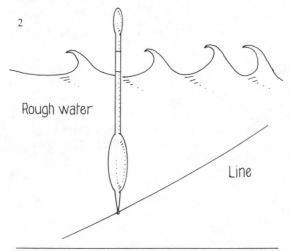

2

Rough water

Line

To some extent, drag can be controlled, but not entirely beaten, by various float attachments. Generally, by using a suitable float, the line can be fastened to it below the surface, which helps to keep the float (and bait) in one position. (2)

The Fish

Size, feeding habits and habitat will govern float selection. This is common-sense although there are anglers who try to compromise with a float entirely unsuited to the species that the angler will *not* be catching!

Under normal circumstances, roach, rudd and dace need a delicate float. Pike require a large, streamlined float that will move away with a fish without it feeling resistance. For grayling, tradition requires a small ducker-type of float designed to cope with the shallow and moving waters these fish inhabit. All these requirements, of course, can be over-ridden by weather conditions and casting distance. (3)

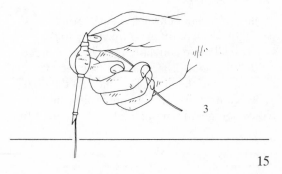

Casting

With floats, size, diameter, weight, shape, all can influence the casting distance, or the way that a cast must be made. But remember, when the float is selected the angler must make sure that the terminal tackle in general (i.e. line, hook link) will be in balance with it. Heavy shotting patterns needed to make bulky floats work can cause havoc with fine nylon. (4)

4

The Light

Near-darkness of dawn and dusk, bright sunlight, the haze of mists that cling to the water – all these and more must be contended with if the float-fisherman wants to see every movement of the float. The shape of the float often controls its visibility but usually the colour of the tip is more likely to be seen. This means changing to a different float, sometimes several times within a short space of time, but it must be done. Light colours against dark backgrounds, special paints, even floats with an illuminated tip, are found in the angler's tackle-box, and with commonsense can be used to good result. (5)

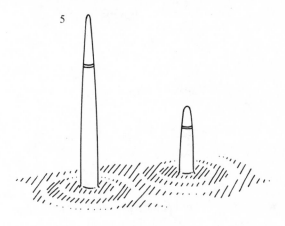

Adaptability

The trap of sticking to one float has been mentioned, and the need of the angler to be prepared to move from one type or colour to another quickly and easily. Some floats allow quick change, some do not. This, therefore, is the time to consider the various means of attaching floats to the line.

- The traditional method of attaching float to line is by means of an eye whipped on to the float's tip. It is certain of doing so, but it also means that shot and hook will have to be removed if a change is to be made, something difficult in poor light conditions. (6)

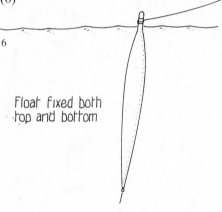

6

Float fixed both top and bottom

- But the eye end can be used to fasten the line to the float so that the depth can be altered easily – simply by taking two turns around the wire, without securing line to the top end. (7)

Line looped

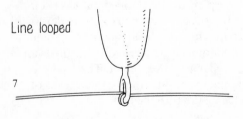

7

- Another possibility with the plain loop is to secure it with two small shot, one either side. Again, this leaves the tip free. (8)

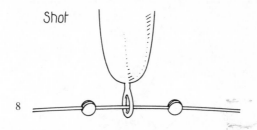

Shot

8

- A commercial quick-release attachment fastens by means of a sliding sleeve to the eye end. Expensive but reliable. (9)

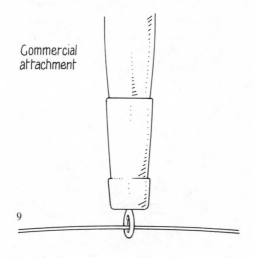

Commercial attachment

9

■ For the d-i-y angler there is the thin wire
held by two pieces of insulating flex. Simple,
cheap, but not foolproof. (10)

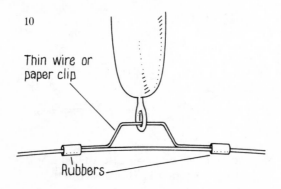

10

Thin wire or
paper clip

Rubbers

■ An improvement on the wire eye is the tiny
swivel that can be embedded in the float's
tip. It prevents line twist – but still remains
difficult to change. (11)

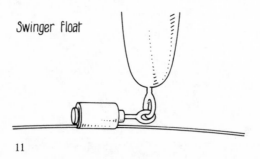

Swinger float

11

■ Float-rubbers are the traditional method of attachment, but they can perish, stretch and slip from the body of the float, thus loosening it. However, many anglers swear by *and at* them. (12)

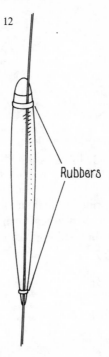

12

Rubbers

■ Moulded sleeves fit over the end of the float stem and provide a quick and easy means of change-over – providing there is room

between the body of the float and the end
of the stem itself. Where quick changes
have to be made it is better than the plain
wire ring. (13)

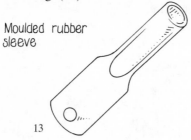

Moulded rubber
sleeve

13

■ The fastest method of float-changing is by
using a spring-clip attachment. This small
wire spring has a loop at one end for the
line. The larger bend at its other end fits
through the ring in the float and the tiny
plastic sleeve then slides down to grip the
spring tight shut. Changes can be made in
seconds. (14)

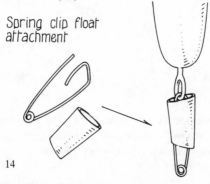

Spring clip float
attachment

14

Storing Floats

Many of today's floats are fragile and need
protection while they are being carried in the
tackle bag — not just from breakage, but from
being chipped and cracked. Many anglers use
cigar-boxes or something similar, but the best
containers are proper padded and sectioned
wooden boxes obtainable from tackle shops:
each float is kept separate from the others and
can be selected quickly. (15)

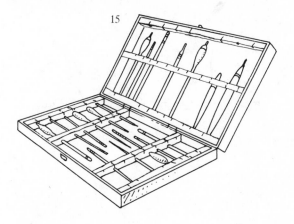

15

Making Floats

Anglers can easily make their own floats. The
tools needed are few, a sharp knife, files, glass-
paper, glue, varnish and paint. Materials are
easily obtainable and inexpensive: balsa wood

and fine dowelling from crafts shop, straws, stiff bristles, tooth-picks, bottle corks — many items are free and plentiful. Feathers can be obtained from farmyards, game dealers, and of course from country walks. There is a range of good float kits on the market supplying ready shaped materials that just need assembling. (16)

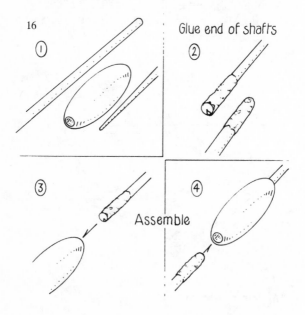

FLOAT PATTERNS

The many shapes and sizes of floats are designed for certain jobs. The principal patterns are listed here with a brief description of the type of fishing they cover.

Quills

- Once the only type of float, quills are the simplest of all and still are among the cheapest and best. They include quills from the swan, goose, duck, crow, pheasant, peacock and porcupine, some you can no longer buy. Those most in use today include the porcupine and the peacock, the latter a favourite because it can be cut into lengths to suit the water. Cork bodies can be added to the quills, making floats capable of carrying a lot of weight. But the value of the simple quill lies in its delicacy, typified by the small crow-quill that can be fixed to the line by either end, and is sensitive enough to record the faint bites from a tench. At the other extreme is the goose quill, often used to make sliding floats for fishing deep water. (17)

Quill floats

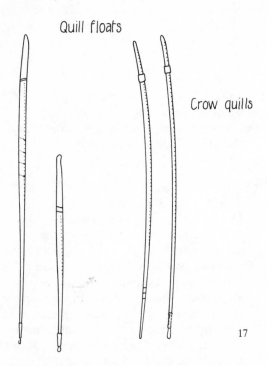

Crow quills

17

Avon Floats

■ Excellent floats for long trotting, in other words allowing the bait to run downstream while pulling line from the reel, with the angler firmly in control and ready to strike.

It takes its name from the River Avon, where the fast flow requires a big, but delicate float. But the Avon float is equally useful on the Thames and Severn. High on the long stem, the balsa body is the secret of this float's success, the weights required to cock it keeping the float well down onto the water. This enables the angler to 'hold back' on the line, keeping the bait in front of the float, not trailing behind, from where it is nearly impossible to register a bite. Even though the float may be lying nearly flat on the surface of the water, the small but sensitive tip above the body will always register the slightest attention. (18)

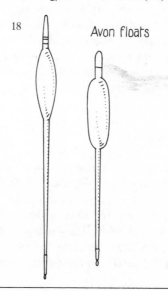

18   Avon floats

Balsa Floats

- These are designed for really tough conditions, rivers that are in flood, or where the deep, boiling water of a swim would play havoc with smaller and more sensitive floats. But the balsa is not insensitive. The secret of sensitivity in any float lies with the size and thickness of that part which protrudes from the surface of the water. And if you look at the balsa family, the tip is small and thin making the slightest touch evident. Nor does size present problems when casting, the streamlined body cutting the air with the minimum of drag. It is possible to cast long distances and still see this all-wood float. Smaller models are very successful in turbulent, shallow water such as parts of weirpools — remaining in view where thinner floats would be sucked under. (19)

Stick Floats

- Designed for running water where there is an even flow, the swim not more than 6 ft deep, stick floats do not work efficiently on waters that are still, slow or very fast. They will cope well with an upstream wind, but fail badly if the wind turns downstream or ruffles the surface of the swim, conditions that drive the float (and the bait) too fast through the swim. Construction includes a balsa body mounted on a thin dowel or cane stem. The stick float is designed so that the tip only shows, the float riding vertically through the swim, when bites are recorded by complete disappearance. (20)

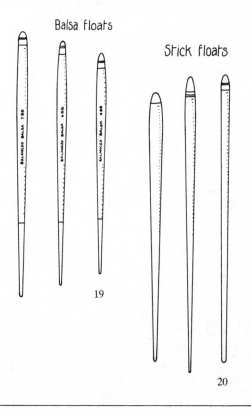

Balsa floats

Stick floats

19

20

- One variation of the stick float uses a wire instead of wood. The wire keeps the float riding easily and in a vertical position, the thin stem keeping water resistance to a minimum and allowing the float to run smoothly through the swim. (21)

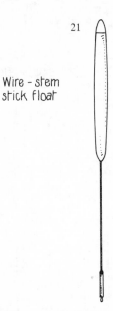

21

Wire - stem stick float

Waggler Floats

- Universal floats, at home on most waters, wagglers are fastened to the line by one end only. They come in all shapes and sizes, the bigger and thicker models being designed to carry more weight. Most wagglers are constructed from peacock-quill stems, bodies being added from cork, balsa, and polystyrene. They are quick and easy to make and provide a good selection for the tackle box. In its plain form the waggler is secured to the line with a shot either side of the end eye, the line being sunk below the surface. (22)

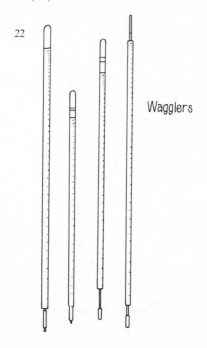

22

Wagglers

■ Variations on the wagglers embody a fat body mounted onto the last third of the stem, which helps to steady it without preventing a delicate bite from being registered. A further advantage of this construction is that is slows the float through the water, keeping the bait moving at a taking speed. (23)

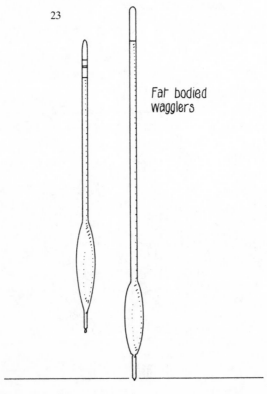

23

Fat bodied wagglers

■ Very large wagglers with enlarged bulbs at
  their end, sometimes over 12 in long, would
  need a mountain of shot to make them
  work. For this reason they are weighted
  with pieces of brass mounted into the body
  and glued into position. Weight on the line
  is kept to a minimum, further weight being
  used with advantage to make extra-long
  casts. (24)

24

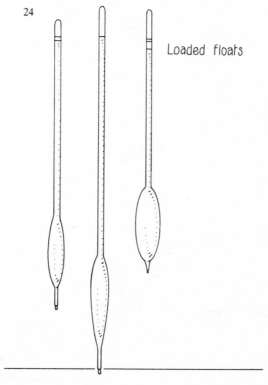

Loaded floats

■ Windbeaters are another branch of the
waggler family used when high winds drive
the waves roaring down the water. Standing
well above the surface, the beacon on the
tip remains relatively steady and helps the
angler to assess a bite. The thin stem slices
through the water making the float very
delicate despite being 10 in or more long.
(25)

Windbeater
float

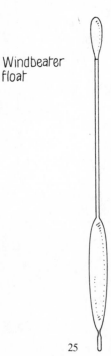

25

Slider Floats

■ For use in deep waters, these floats, as the
name suggests, slide down the line until a
predetermined place is reached where a
stop knot has been set, preventing further
sinking of the bait and cocking the float.
Many anglers use an ordinary float, setting
the stop knot so that it will be held at the
end ring, and attaching the float to the line
by that loop only. But this method is not as
successful as the float properly constructed
to slide. Remember that the slider can
present a bait both on and off the bottom.
(26)

26

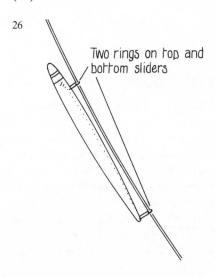

Two rings on top and
bottom sliders

- The sliding float is only successful when the correct stop knot has been used. This diagram shows how it should be tied. (27)

Stop knot

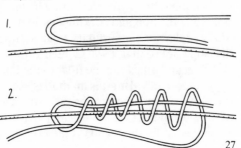

27

Antennae Floats

- These are great floats for general fishing where there is movement on the water. The thin stick that cuts the surface is unmoved as waves pass over it but because of the balance of the body, the float — and the bait — remains still and not bobbing up and down. It is from this float, one of angling's golden oldies, that the waggler developed. Unlike the waggler, attached at the bottom end only, this float is fastened at top and bottom. (28)

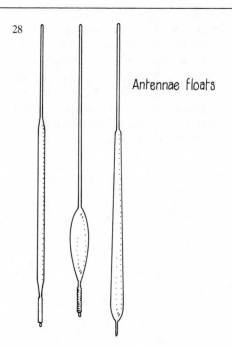

28

Antennae floats

Bubble Floats

■ These are transparent, plastic bubbles that
have a small hole sealed with a plug in the
side allowing them to be filled with water,
making weight for casting. Originally
designed for use when fly fishing, the bubble
float lay on the surface and acted as a
controller for the fly which could be
manoeuvred into positions not normally
reached. In coarse fishing it is used in very

shallow water, or positions where the
normal float, with part of its body lying
under the surface, would arouse suspicion.
Line passes through the two eyed loops at
either end, and allows the float to be pushed
up and down in the same way as a normal
float. Useful where long distance is needed,
yet freelining at the same time. (29)

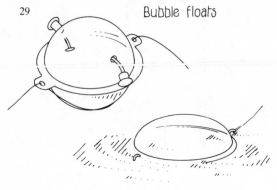

29   Bubble floats

Streamlined bubble float

Pole Floats

- Designed for use with ultra fine lines and
  hooks, pole floats are strong weapons in the
  match-angler's armoury. Adopted from the
  Continent, pole floats feature a strong and
  rather outsized body which gives stability
  for casting and, sunk below the surface,

hold the bait steady. Their needle-fine stems can just be seen as a tiny whisker protruding through the surface, presenting no resistance to a taking fish and recording the most delicate of bites. (30)

30   Continental pole floats

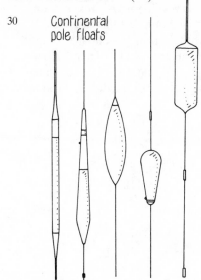

■ Because pole floats are so delicate, anglers make them up at home and transport them on plastic winders ready for mounting or changing as required. (31)

31

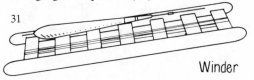

Winder

Night Lights

■ There have been various attempts at
producing a float that can be seen during
night fishing. But the best is probably the
Betanyte, which houses a tiny tritium-
powered light tip that lasts for years, and
glows with a strong light no matter how
dark the night might be. There are similar
models on the market, all on the same
principle. Float fishing during darkness is

32

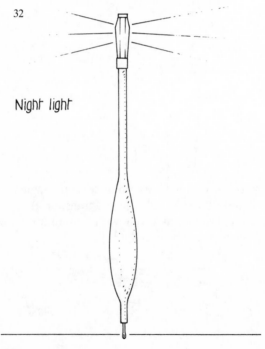

Night light

not easy, the float can often be taken away
by a slowly moving fish without the angler
being aware of it. This float is at its best
when seen against a contrasting background
when movement can be seen. (32)

Bungs

- Originally the leading float for pike anglers,
  the bung has now been eclipsed by modern,
  streamlined models that do not present its
  resistance to a taking fish. The *Fishing
  Gazette* model led the field for years and is
  still available. (33)

Fishing Gazette
float

Removable peg

33

- Modern pike floats are mostly sliders called
  'cigars' for obvious reasons, the line being
  led through the centre of the float's body

and stopped by a stop knot. The type of water and the size of the bait govern the size of the float. (34)

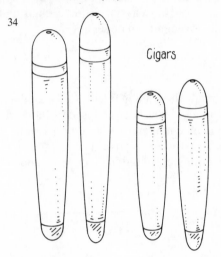

34

Cigars

- Some pike men believe that the use of a tiny pilot float gives less resistance to a taking fish and these are popular. (35)

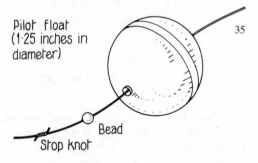

Pilot float
(1·25 inches in
diameter)

35

Bead

Stop knot

WEIGHTS FOR FLOAT FISHING

Weight is necessary when float fishing to make it stand up and show above the surface, and to help in making a cast. The amount needed depends on the type of water to be fished, the float that has been selected and the style of fishing decided upon. Until recently the line was weighted by lead shot, but legislation now prevents its use because of allegations that it poisons bird life. Under the Control of Pollution (Anglers' Lead Weights) Regulations 1986 the importation and sale of lead weights below 1oz was prohibited, and the angler's traditional split-shot usage was no more. There are now a number of substitutes on the market with the mass and appearance of the traditional lead shot and where the terms 'split shot', 'shot' or 'lead(s)' are used these refer to lead substitutes and not traditional lead shot.

- Shot for weighting the line is split, allowing it to be cramped together. Softness is essential or it will damage the line as it is squeezed. Examine and select the best of

the artificial lead substitutes that are
available in the tackle shop. (36)

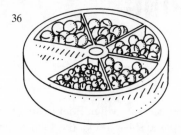

- Shot is sized, the numbers used to describe
  the size running in descending order. The
  same method of shot description is used by
  those who shoot, so some of their
  terminology has crept into angling. Biggest
  is swan-shot, followed by AAA, BB, No. 4,
  6, 8 and so on. Size 10 is probably the
  smallest, but there are some smaller still —
  usually used in pole fishing. (37)

Split shot (actual size)

		Number per ounce		
SSG	15	170	4
AAA	35	220	5
BB	70	270	6
1	100	340	7
3	140	450	8

37

■ Most modern floats have the weight needed
to cock them marked along the body,
otherwise trial and error have to find the
shot required to make the float work. (38)

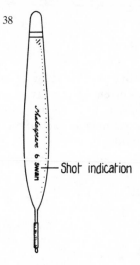

Shot indication

Weighting Patterns

■ Attaching shot on to the line in any order or
position is bad fishing and will not make the
float work properly. There is no guarantee
that the bait will be where it should be, and
it could even restrict the distance of the
cast. Patterns, the placing of shot, are
important and the principal ones are
introduced in the next chapter, with an
explanation of the various fishing styles.

FLOAT-FISHING STYLES

The float can be used in stillwater or in the flow of the current and the styles described here are those well-proven traditional methods found to be suitable for the varying conditions the angler finds.

39

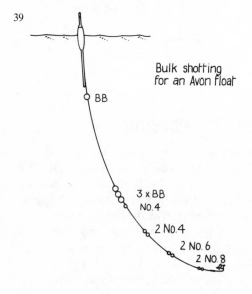

Bulk shotting
for an Avon float

BB

3 x BB
NO. 4

2 No. 4

2 No. 6

2 No. 8

Trotting

■ A general term that describes a bait carried along with the current. Another description is swimming the stream. The bait must precede the float or a bite will not register. The shotting pattern for use with the Avon float is shown. (39)

■ A trotting pattern for water with a slower flow is shown, using a stick float. (40)

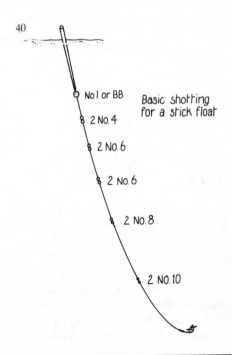

40

No l or BB

2 No. 4

2 No. 6

2 No. 6

2 No. 8

2 No. 10

Basic shotting for a stick float

■ Where the water moves quickly but strong
wind is creating a fast drag across the
surface, use this pattern with a large
waggler. (41)

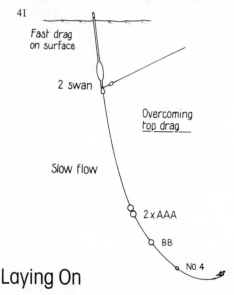

41

Fast drag
on surface

2 swan

Overcoming
top drag

Slow flow

2 x AAA

BB

NO. 4

Laying On

■ In this style, the bait is allowed to lay on the
bottom and is kept there with a small weight
while the float lies at an angle, ready to
record the smallest bite, the line between it
and the bottom shot tight. Almost any float
can be used for this rig which is usually
practised in stationary or slow-moving
water. Here the rig shows a waggler,
fastened at the bottom end only which

allows the line to be sunk below the surface,
an assistance in avoiding drag where there
is any wind. (42)

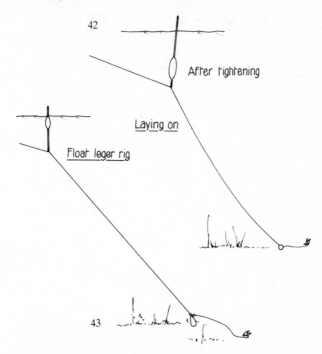

42

After tightening

Laying on

Float leger rig

43

■ Another method of laying on, float-
legering, uses a leger weight instead of a
small shot on the bottom. This rig allows
long casting and is delicate and responsive
to bites in spite of its rather clumsy
appearance. (43)

Stret-Pegging

■ This is a style of laying on with the angler
using the current to work the bait round
from just in front, to a position against the
bank downstream of his swim. The rod must
constantly be held because bites are often
fast — sometimes with such force that fish
practically hook themselves. The ordinary
Avon rig is used but the float is adjusted so
that the length between it and the hook is
greater than the depth to be fished. This
keeps the bait scraping the river bed at all
times. (44)

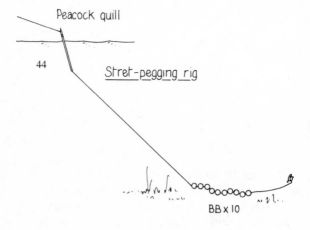

Peacock quill

44

Stret-pegging rig

BB x 10

Lift Method

■ By attaching a float by the end only and
keeping weight to a minimum a float will lift
and lay it on its side when a fish takes the
bait. It is done by having the largest shot
just resting on the bottom and keeping a
short link between it and the bait. An
excellent stillwater rig. (45)

45

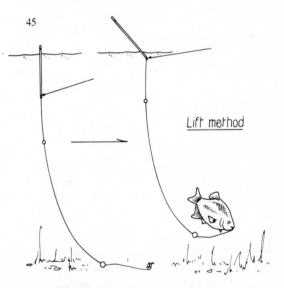

Lift method

When the bait is taken, the bottom
weight is lifted and the float rises

Drop Method

■ Allowing the bait to sink slowly in still
waters is a certain way of catching roach,
rudd and similar species. A tiny waggler
cocked by the finest shot will allow that
slow drop of the bait that fish cannot resist.
(46)

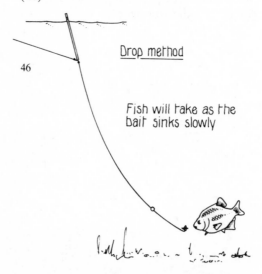

Drop method

46

Fish will take as the
bait sinks slowly

■ Drop-fishing needs careful groundbaiting, a
cloud groundbait gets the best results. Be
careful not to make the cloud groundbait
too much of a feed, thus spoiling the
chances of the hookbait. Any kind of
groundbait must attract — not feed the fish.
(47)

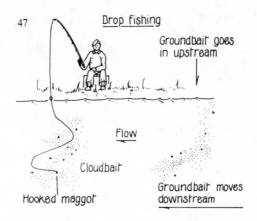

47 <u>Drop fishing</u>

Groundbait goes
in upstream

Flow

Cloudbait

Hooked maggot

Groundbait moves
downstream

■ Try sinking the bait quickly after a period of
drop fishing, because bigger fish may be
below those that you are catching. This
shotting pattern will get the bait down past
smaller fish in double-quick time. (48)

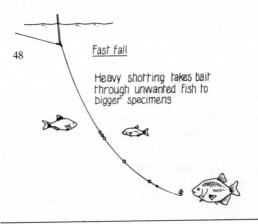

48 <u>Fast fall</u>

Heavy shotting takes bait
through unwanted fish to
bigger specimens

■ The drop method can be used in running
water with good effect. This slow-sinking
rig using an Avon float shows how to fish it.
(49)

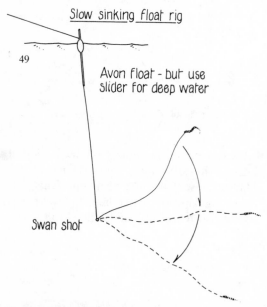

Slow sinking float rig

49

Avon float - but use
slider for deep water

Swan shot

Sink-and-Draw

■ Sink-and-draw is a method of attracting the
fish by moving the bait instead of waiting
for a fish to find it. Instead of a float, one
shot is pinched on to the line above the bait
with enough weight to enable a cast to be
made. The bait is allowed to sink and then

worked back to the angler in a series of
jerks. (50)

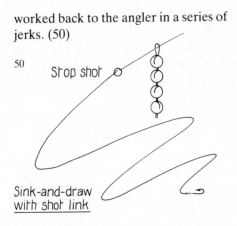

⁵⁰ Stop shot

Sink-and-draw
with shot link

■ Another method of sink-and-draw is by the
use of a bubble float. This assists bite
detection through movement from the float.
But with the sink-and-draw style the best
bite detection is by feel. (51)

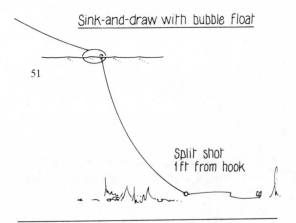

Sink-and-draw with bubble float

51

Split shot
1ft from hook

Sliding-Float Rigs

- Fishing the bait off the bottom demands the
  shot pattern to be well above the bait. This
  rig is using a waggler secured through the
  end ring only. (52)

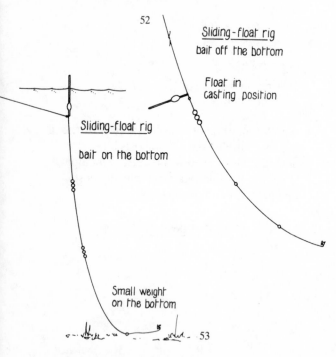

52

Sliding-float rig
bait off the bottom

Float in
casting position

Sliding-float rig

bait on the bottom

Small weight
on the bottom

53

- For fishing with the bait on the bottom, the
  shot pattern is split with one shot resting on
  the bed. (53)

Stick Floats

■ Many anglers kill the sensitivity of this float
  by using too much weight. In shotting with
  the stick the secret is 'small and plenty', as
  this diagram of a representative stick-float
  rig shows. (54)

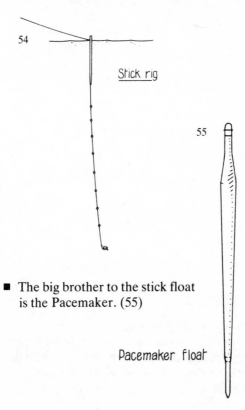

54

Stick rig

55

■ The big brother to the stick float
  is the Pacemaker. (55)

Pacemaker float

■ A heavyweight for heavy water conditions,
the shotting pattern for the Pacemaker takes
time to put in place, but keeps the bait
down. (56)

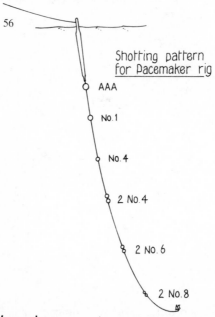

56

Shotting pattern
for Pacemaker rig

AAA

No. 1

No. 4

2 No. 4

2 No. 6

2 No. 8

Wagglers

■ Wagglers are secured by the ring end only.
One possible method is by using a dust shot
each side of the ring itself. But care must be
taken or the float won't pull under on the
bite. The incorrect way is shown here, with

the shots close against the ring, preventing movement of the float to indicate a bite. (57)

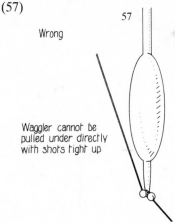

57

Wrong

Waggler cannot be pulled under directly with shots right up

■ The correct way, leaving a gap between the shot and the float allows it to hang and dip when the bait is taken. (58)

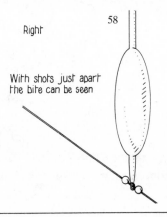

58

Right

With shots just apart the bite can be seen

■ This shot pattern allows a slow-sinking bait, often taken by fish as it falls. (59)

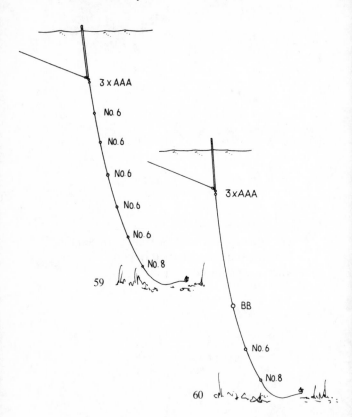

■ For a more rapid sinking of the bait use this pattern, concentrating weight at the bottom end. (60)

■ Buoyant baits, such as crust, will need even more weight to keep them on the bottom. This shotting pattern is ideal for the purpose. (61)

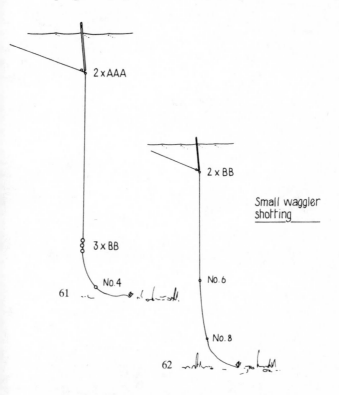

2 x AAA

2 x BB

Small waggler shotting

3 x BB

No. 4

No. 6

61

No. 8

62

■ For very confined waters that require small floats this shotting pattern is recommended. (62)

■ Occasionally it is necessary to slow a bait
down while swimming the stream. This
pattern trails the bait and holds back the
float. (63)

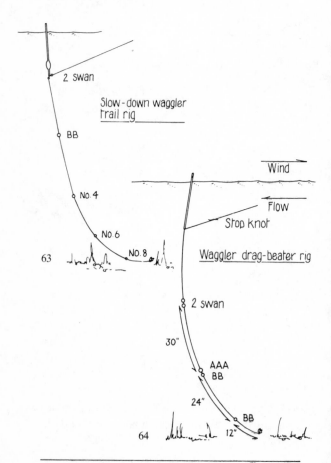

Slow-down waggler
trail rig

Waggler drag-beater rig

- When the wind is against the current a drag is created which causes the float to ride around on the surface. Here is a pattern and style to combat those conditions. (64)

Float Paternoster

- A deadly way of anchoring a bait in one position and keeping it off the bottom. It is usual'y used with a small livebait for perch and fished roving-style, the angler moving along the bank casting into likely places. (65)

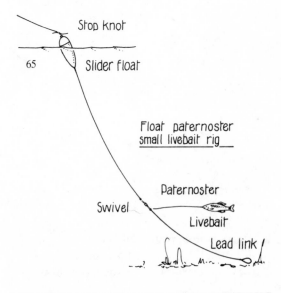

Stop knot

65   Slider float

Float paternoster
small livebait rig

Paternoster

Swivel   Livebait

Lead link

Pole Float Rigs

■ Shotting these tiny floats is an art in itself. The weights are minute and there is a special cramp for fastening them to the line. The larger sizes, called Olivetti leads, are usually pear shaped and hollow so they can be threaded down the line. Other small leger weights are Styl leads and Mouse Droppings (because of their unpleasant resemblance in shape and size!). They are less likely to tangle than strings of shot. (66)

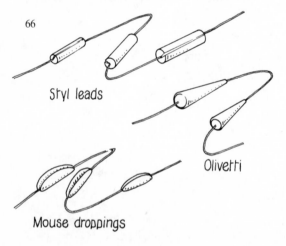

66

Styl leads

Olivetti

Mouse droppings

■ The pole float is shotted until the fine stem just breaks the water. Two methods of shotting are shown, one for a Teardrop

float, the other for what is known as a
Carrot. (67, 68)

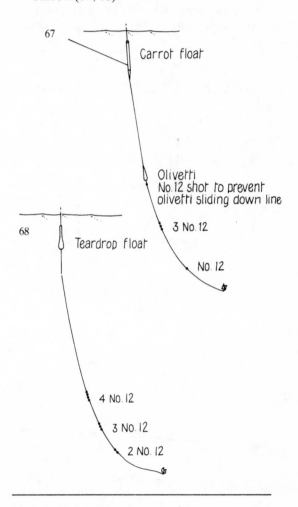

67   Carrot float

Olivetti
No.12 shot to prevent
olivetti sliding down line

3 No. 12

No. 12

68   Teardrop float

4 No. 12

3 No. 12

2 No. 12

■ It takes time to shot these floats correctly.
The best way of doing it is with the aid of a
bucket of water at home, and not on the
river bank. (69)

69

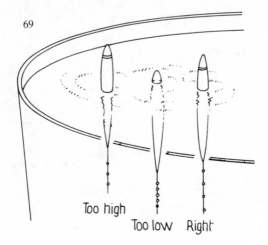

Too high

Too low   Right

SWIMFEEDERS

These are plastic cylinders that are weighted, and either open at both ends or closed (called block-ends) and can be attached to the line and used to place groundbait by the hook-bait where it is needed. There are a number of models on the market.

■ Open-end feeders are secured to the line by a loop. They are packed with groundbait which is washed free in the current. (70)

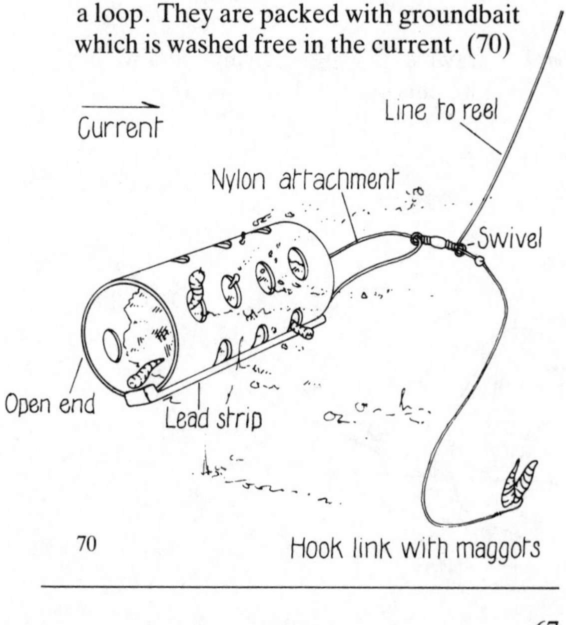

Current

Line to reel

Nylon attachment

Swivel

Open end

Lead strip

70

Hook link with maggots

- Block-end feeders can be used to hold maggots that wriggle and wash free into the swim. (71)

Block-end swimfeeder

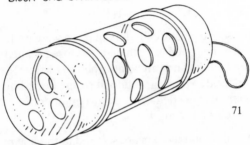

71

- Use a swivel to fasten a swimfeeder to the line; it helps prevent line kink. (72)

72

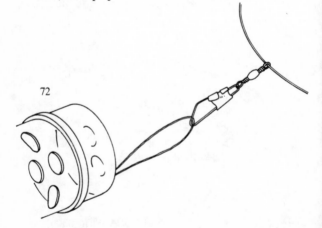

■ The swimfeeder takes the place of the
weight when float-legering, but it is more
usual to use it with the pure leger rig. (73)

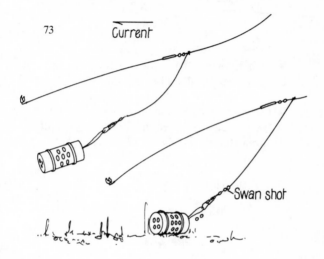

73 Current

Swan shot

PIKE-FISHING RIGS

Whether you are live or deadbaiting, three
basic rigs are used in pike fishing.

- Unless you are fishing in very shallow water,
  the live or suspended deadbait rig is usually
  supported by a sliding float. (74)

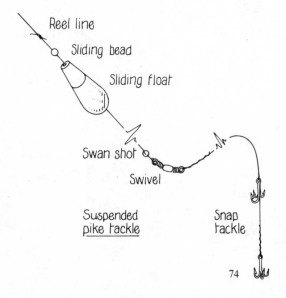

Reel line

Sliding bead

Sliding float

Swan shot

Swivel

Suspended
pike tackle

Snap
tackle

74

- The paternostered live or deadbait rig is similar to that used for perch but with stronger tackle. (75)

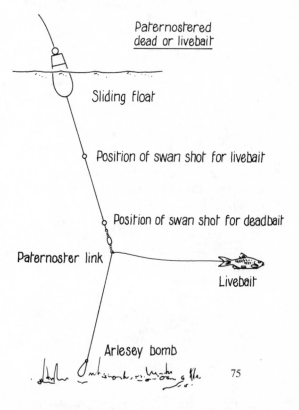

Paternostered
dead or livebait

Sliding float

Position of swan shot for livebait

Position of swan shot for deadbait

Paternoster link

Livebait

Arlesey bomb

75

- The float-leger is another popular pike rig, most anglers using the sunken-float method which keeps the line clear of the bottom

and stops it drifting. A useful rig where
there are known to be snags. (76)

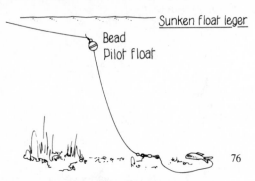

Sunken float leger

Bead
Pilot float

76

■ Some anglers prefer to troll using a float. It
helps keep the bait at a pre-determined
depth. (77)

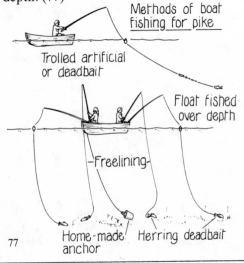

Methods of boat
fishing for pike

Trolled artificial
or deadbait

Float fished
over depth

—Freelining—

Home-made
anchor

Herring deadbait

77

LEGER RIGS

More difficult than float-fishing, legering means presenting a bait without the use of a float. Bites are harder to detect and analyse and there is little help from the water to manoeuvre a bait. But with practice it is possible to estimate what a fish is doing to the bait by vibrations transmitted back along the line and rod tip to the angler. It is also possible in running water to work the bait into areas that cannot be reached by casting.

Why and where do you use the leger? When weather conditions are so bad that using a float would be impossible, and where the sheer expanse of water is too big to cast with light tackle. But modern legering is not a matter of using heavy weight and long casts. One can leger on stillwaters and present a bait with great accuracy and delicacy. To do that it is necessary to know about the weights used in legering.

Leger Weights

It is now illegal to use lead in weights smaller
than 1oz (see page 43) and anything lighter
must be one of the lead substitutes. Some
anglers made their own shot but the new
legislation largely prevents this.

- As the name suggests, coffin leads are
  shaped like a coffin with a hole bored
  through the centre. Being flat they do not
  move around once they touch bottom, and
  are used for fast-flowing waters such as
  weir-pools and places where it is necessary
  to keep the bait stationary. (78)

78

Coffin leads

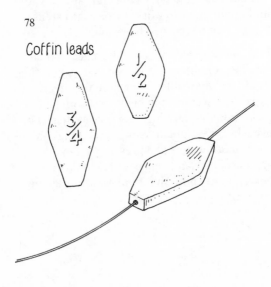

- The Arlesey bomb was designed by the late, famous Richard Walker for use in exceptionally deep waters — principally gravel pits. He wanted the lead to sink without twisting the line, and to sink in a straight line. The pear shape and in-built swivel of this leger lead was the perfect answer. (79)

79   Arlesey bombs

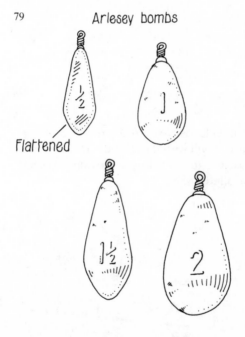

Flattened

- Barrel leads — sometimes called barleycorns — are long and cylindrical.

Able to roll but not to turn end to end, they are occasionally used as searching leger rigs. (80)

Barrel leads

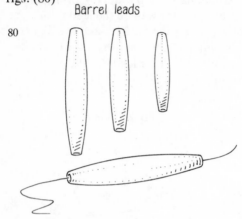

80

■ Bullet leads are perfectly round, and can roll at will with the current. The angler can use this to advantage in moving the bait around. (81)

Bullet leads

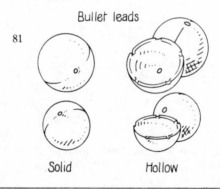

81

Solid   Hollow

■ Swimfeeders can be purchased with
different shapes and weights in the form of
strip metal fastened along their length. They
not only provide weight for casting, but
groundbait at the same time. (82)

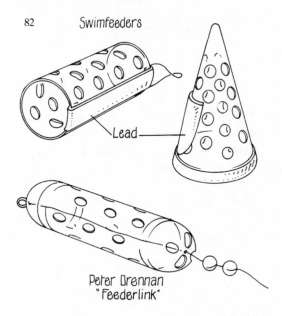

82   Swimfeeders

Lead

Peter Drennan
"Feederlink"

Leger Stops

To stop the weight from sliding down the line
to the hook it is necessary to have a stop. There
are various forms.

- The matchstick secured by two half-hitches is universal when using a bullet lead. It allows line to pull free without friction. (83)

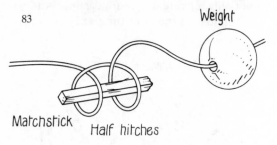

83

Weight

Matchstick   Half hitches

- The crimped split-shot is often used — but this can damage the line if crimped too tightly with the pliers, or slide down the line if not tight enough. (84)

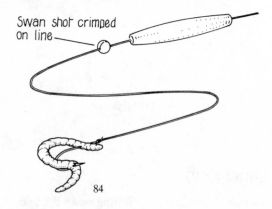

Swan shot crimped on line

84

- Swivel stops are popular and work well. But they do not stop the weight from putting a

twist in the line. To prevent that it is
necessary to have a second swivel mounted
above the lead itself. (85)

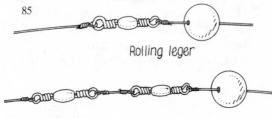

85

Rolling leger

Two swivels help
avoid line twist

■ Leger stops purchased at the tackle shop
are fool-proof and worth the money. They
are not easy to find if dropped in grass or
mud, so buy several packets at a time. (86)

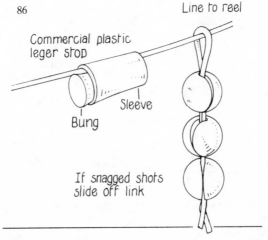

86

Line to reel

Commercial plastic
leger stop

Sleeve

Bung

If snagged shots
slide off link

Static Leger

■ In this style the angler attaches sufficient
lead in the line to hold the bottom, and casts
in front of the swim, keeping the rod in its
rests and a tight line between line and lead.
The smallest attention from a fish will
register by movement of the rod tip. (87)

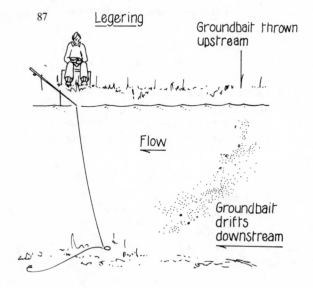

87 Legering

Groundbait thrown
upstream

Flow

Groundbait
drifts
downstream

Rolling Leger

- A pierced bullet, stopped by a matchstick, allows the current to roll and move both weight and bait. A good tip is to enlarge the hole at the ends of the bullet so that line is not trapped. (88)

88 Rolling leger in running water

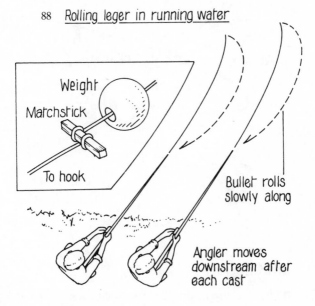

Weight

Matchstick

To hook

Bullet rolls slowly along

Angler moves downstream after each cast

Long-range Leger

- The streamlined Arlesey bomb together
  with the use of a swivel and protective
  rubber float-cap make this rig ideal for
  really long-distance casting. Use baits that
  stay on the hook while casting — lobworms
  are ideal. (89)

Long-range leger

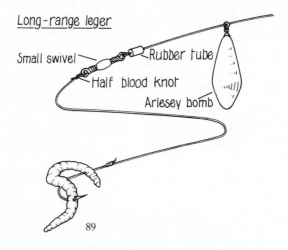

Small swivel — Rubber tube
— Half blood knot
Arlesey bomb

89

Link Leger

- The feature of this leger is a split ring,
  stopped when the cast is made by the hook
  eye but which allows the bait to run free
  once the rig reaches the bottom. The link
  also helps to prevent a fish feeling resistance
  when picking up the bait. (90)

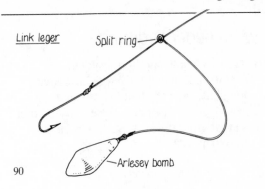

Link leger   Split ring

Arlesey bomb

90

Fixed-link Leger

■ An easy rig to use on a cold day when frozen
  fingers will not cope with fine tackle. The
  use of two link swivels means that the hook-
  link or the leger weight can be changed
  instantly. (91)

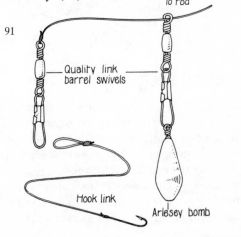

To rod

91

Quality link
barrel swivels

Hook link   Arlesey bomb

83

Swimfeeder Legering

- This is a deadly method, using the swimfeeder instead of a weight. Leave a long link, with the baited hook and swimfeeder reasonably close to each other so that groundbait brings fish close to the hookbait. (92)

92 Swimfeeder legering

Flow

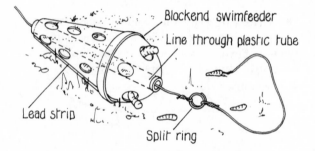

Blockend swimfeeder

Line through plastic tube

Lead strip

Split ring

Paper-bag Legering

- The use of a paper bag to hold groundbait where the swim is not too distant and can be reached by gentle casting is one method of groundbaiting and weighting at the same time. As the bag falls apart the bait is released — and the hookbait is also allowed to run free. The rig shown is for eels, but it can apply equally to other species. (93)

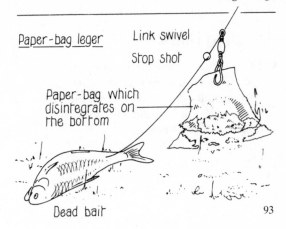

Paper-bag leger

Link swivel

Stop shot

Paper-bag which disintegrates on the bottom

Dead bait

93

Swan-shot Legering

■ Swan shot clipped to a link of nylon looped over the reel line makes a delicate rig for any fish. Weight can be added or removed in an instant. (94)

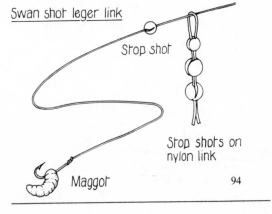

Swan shot leger link

Stop shot

Stop shots on nylon link

Maggot

94

Detecting Bites

■ There are many ways of detecting the bite
of a taking fish, some simple, some
complicated as here. Whichever method
you use, for success and a hooked fish every
time the secret is practice.
(95)

95

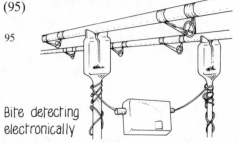

Bite detecting
electronically

Touch Legering

■ With this style, the rod is held in the hand
and the line between lead and rod kept taut
so that the angler can feel taps as a fish

96

attacks the bait. Touch-legering is especially useful when fishing fast waters for barbel. (96)

Rod Rests

- With the rod supported in rests so that it cannot move, any bite will be recorded at the tip. The angler must be seated so that he can pick the rod up immediately and there should be a high ratio of hooked fish to bites. A piece of folded silver paper pinched on to the line below the rod tip will indicate bites. (97, 98)

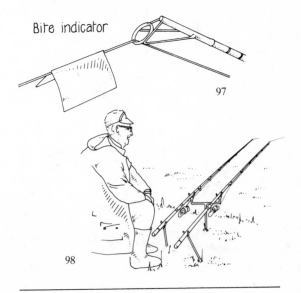

Bite indicator

97

98

Butt Indicators

■ If the rod is held in two rests, the line can be
looped through a rubber band, or weighted
by a ball of paste squeezed onto the line
between reel and first rod ring. In either
case a taking fish will pull line and either
slide it from the bands or lift the paste ball.
(99)

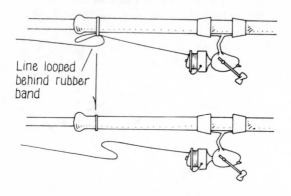

Line looped
behind rubber
band

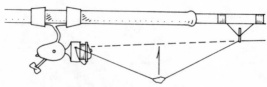

Ball of paste pinched to line which
straightens when fish takes

99

Swingtips

■ Useful on stillwaters, this rod tip extension
is screwed into the end ring of the rod lying
at right-angles to the water. Attention from
a fish will lift it — the movement depending
on the strength of the bite. (100)

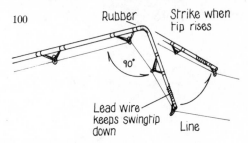

100   Rubber   Strike when
                                    tip rises

90°

Lead wire
keeps swingtip
down   Line

Quivertips

■ It is better to use a quivertip where the
current is strong. The stiff, small joint
screws into the end ring of the rod in the
same way as the swingtip but remains
straight. With the rod adjusted in its rests
the sensitive quiver-tip records the tiniest
touch from a fish. (101)

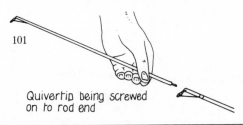

101

Quivertip being screwed
on to rod end

■ An aid many anglers employ to recognise
small bites is the use of a board to isolate
the quivertip from the background of water
or bank. The indicator-board can be plain,
coloured, or marked with a target. (102)

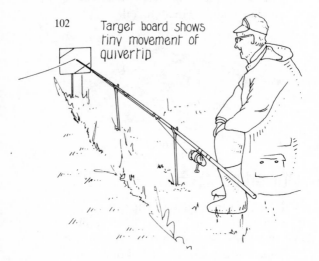

102   Target board shows
tiny movement of
quivertip

INDEX

A

Adaptability, in floats 17
Antennae floats 36
Arlesey bomb 75, 82
Attachments for floats 21
moulded sleeves 21
Avon floats 26

B

Balsa floats 27, 28, 31
Barleycorn leads 75
Barrel leads 75
Betanyte 40
Block-ends 67
Bream 10
Bubble floats 37, 55
Bullet leads 76, 81
Bungs 41
Butt (bite) indicators 88

C

Carrot float 65
Casting 16
  with floats 16
'Cigar' floats 41
Coffin leads 74

D

Dace 10, 15
Deadbaiting 70
Detecting bites 10
Drop method 52
Drop fishing 52

E

Eyes, of floats 18

F

Fishing Gazette bung 41
Fish species
  bream 10
  dace 10, 15
  grayling 15
  perch 10
  pike 11, 15, 41
  roach 15, 52
  rudd 15, 52
  tench 10, 25
Fixed-link leger 83
Floats
  adaptability 17
  antennae floats 36
  as focal point 9
  attaching to line 18

Avon floats 26, 47, 50, 54
balsa floats 27, 28, 31
Betanyte 40
bubble floats 37, 55
bungs 41
carrot float 65
'cigar' floats 41
colour 16
cork-bodied floats 25, 31
crow quills 25
drag 15
duck quills 25
duckers 15
eyes 18
Fishing Gazette bung 41
float-fishing styles 46
float leger 9, 49, 71
float movements 10, 16
float paternoster 63
float patterns 25
float rubbers 21, 83
floats for long-trotting 26
goose quills 25
illuminated floats 17
in current 11, 28
in wind 11, 28
laying-on 48
making floats 23
moulded sleeves 21
night lights 40

Pacemaker 57
patterns 25
peacock quills 25
pheasant quills 25
pike floats 41
pilot floats 42
plastic winders 39
pole floats 38, 65
polystyrene 31
porcupine quills 25
quick-release attachments 19
quills 25
recording bites 10, 11
shape 16
slider floats 35, 41, 56, 71
spring-clip attachments 22
stick floats 23, 28, 47, 57
storing 23
swan quills 25
trotting 47
waggler floats 30, 36, 48, 52, 58
weights, for float fishing 43, 44
windbeater floats 14, 34
with swivels for attachment 20
Float-fishing styles 46
drop method 52

laying on 48
leger 9, 49
lift method 51
paternoster 83
sink-and-draw 54
stret-pegging 50
trotting 47
Float leger(ing) 9, 49
Float movements 10, 16
Float paternoster 63
Float quills 25
Float rubbers 21
Float sensitivity 26

L
Laying-on 48
Lead shot 43
    Control of Pollution
        Regulations 43
    lead substitutes 74
    prohibition 43
    sizes 44
Lead substitutes 74
Leger rigs 73
    butt indicators 88
    detecting bites 73, 86
    fixed-link leger 83
    link-leger 82
    long-range leger 82
    on stillwaters 73
    paper-bag leger 84
    rod-rests 87
    rolling leger 81
    static leger 80
    swan-shot leger 85

swimfeeder leger 84
touch legering 86
why and where? 73
Leger stops 77-79
    matchsticks 78
    split shots 78
    swivel stops 78
Leger weights 74
    Arlesey bombs 75
    barleycorn leads 75
    barrel leads 75
    bullet leads 76
    coffin leads 74
    lead substitutes 74
    swimfeeders 77
Lift method 51
Light 16
Link-leger 82
Livebaiting 70
Lobworms 82
Long-range leger 82
Long-trotting floats 26

M
Making floats 23
    balsa wood 23
    bristles 24
    corks 24
    dowelling 24
    feathers 24
    files 23
    glass-paper 23
    glue 23
    knife 23
    requirements 23, 24

straw 24
tooth-picks 24
varnish 23
Moulded-sleeves, for
    float attachment 21
Mouse-droppings
    (weights) 64

N
Night lights (floats) 40

O
Olivetti leads 64

P
Pacemaker 57
Paper-bag leger 84
Perch 10
Pike 11, 15, 41
Pike-fishing rigs 70
Pike floats 70
Pilot floats 42
Pole floats 38, 65

Q
Quick-release
    attachments, for
    floats 19
Quills 25
    crow 25
    duck 25
    goose 25, 26
    peacock 25
    pheasant 25
    porcupine 25
    swan 25

Quivertips 89
    indicator board 90

R
Rain 14
Recording bites 10, 11
Rod-rests 87
Rolling leger 81

S
Shot (see Lead Shot)
Shotting patterns 16,
    46-66
Sink-and-draw 54
Slider floats 26, 35, 41
Slider float rigs 56
Split shot (see Lead
    Shot)
Spring-clip
    attachments, for
    floats 22
Static leger 80
Stick floats 23, 28, 47, 57
Stick float rigs 47
Storing floats 23
Stret-pegging 50
Styl leads 64
Swan-shot leger 85
Swimfeeders 67, 77
    block-ends 67
    open-ends 67
Swimfeeder leger 77, 84
Swimming the stream
    11, 47
Swingtips 89

T
Teardrop float 65
Tench 10
Trolling 72
Trotting 47

V
Visibility 14

W
Waggler floats 30, 36, 48, 52, 58
  weighted with brass 33
Water 12
  movement 12
Weather 14, 15
  colour 13

light 14
rain 14
wind 14
Weights (see also Lead shot) 43
Weighting patterns 45
  drop method (style) 52
  float paternoster 63
  laying-on 48
  leger weights 74
  lift method 51
  sink-and-draw 54
  stret-pegging 50
  trotting 47
  wagglers 30, 36, 48, 52, 54
Wind 14
Windbeater floats 14, 34